Journey to Joy

Discovering God's Love in Real Time

T0171417

Joyce Strong

iUniverse, Inc.

New York Bloomington

Journey to Joy
Discovering God's Love in Real Time

iUniverse books may be ordered through booksellers or by contacting:

iUniverse
1663 Liberty Drive
Bloomington, IN 47403
www.iuniverse.com
1-800-Authors (1-800-288-4677)

Because of the dynamic nature of the Internet, any Web addresses or links contained in this book may have changed since publication and may no longer be valid.

ISBN: 978-1-4502-4792-4 (sc)
ISBN: 978-1-4502-4794-8 (ebk)

Printed in the United States of America

iUniverse rev. date: 9/21/2010

Dedicated to the courageous men and women
who seek true Joy...

Table of Contents

Introduction

It was a beautiful spring day, full of life and promise. The birds were back in Blendon Woods, and the wild flowers were just beginning to bloom along the path. I stopped beside a deep ravine and leaned against the railing that protected me from tumbling down the steep, rocky slope to the stream bed below.

An ancient tree just beyond the fence caught my eye. Carved into its bark were the initials of countless precious people who had passed that way. I sensed God drawing my attention to them.

As I studied that tree and thought of the many lives represented by those initials, the words of Isaiah 49:16 flashed through my mind. I could imagine God holding out His hand to me saying, "*See? I have written* **your** *name on the palm of my hand.*"

He knows us and loves us. Our names are not written on a tree that will someday rot and return to the earth. They are written on the hand of our Creator and Eternal God.

This God now invites us on a *Journey to Joy*. On this journey, we will find ourselves as we were meant to be when He created us. As we trust Him and obey His counsel, our hearts and relationships will be healed, and we will learn how to love the way He loves us. And all the while, He will be our dearest friend and wonderful Savior. We will come to know personally the Creator who has a unique design for our lives.

Get ready for *Joy!*

Part 1

Becoming Who We Were Created to Be

Chapter One

Given New Hearts

Welcome to the *Journey to Joy!* Together we will experience God's love and come to cherish His presence more than anything else. Even when we travel through difficult and dangerous places, He will turn our tears and pain into strength and deep-seated joy.

We will be changed.

I love David's words in Psalm 84:5-7, New Living Translation: *Happy are those who are strong in the Lord, who set their minds on a pilgrimage to Jerusalem (God's presence). When they walk through the Valley of Weeping, it will become a place of refreshing springs, where pools of blessing collect after the rains. They will continue to grow stronger, and each of them will appear before God in Jerusalem.*

Every journey has a starting place. For us, it will be where our need for God began, deep in our pasts. Shall we begin?

Our Histories

Everyone has a life story. It is a story of not only our past joys and sorrows, but also our hopes and dreams. We bring that story into our journey with God.

Within that story, there are usually areas that need to be healed by Jesus before we are whole and truly who we were created to be. Here's a little of *my* life story:

I grew up on a farm in Western New York State. My parents were strong Christians and leaders in our small hometown church. I invited Jesus into my heart and life when I was only five years old. I remember the joy of telling my friends about Jesus as we were growing up. I led one of them to the Lord while we were sitting high up on a beam in my father's barn.

On lazy, summer afternoons, my dog Ginger and I would follow the creek into the woods, and then wander out into the open fields on the hillside far above our farmhouse. There, we would find a soft spot in the hayfield and I'd lie on my back, searching the skies for the face of Jesus. How I longed for Him to return right then! I imagined Him bursting through the clouds at any moment.

It was a wonderful childhood free of fear and full of love. But as I moved into my teen years, new pressures came to bear on my young life that would take my eyes off the skies and have big consequences later:

• The message that I received from my parents and my church was that God's reputation depended upon my behavior. I had to dress a certain way, act a certain way, and never make a mistake. Any flaw or weakness in my life, I concluded, must be kept a secret.

•   My mother praised me effusively to others. As a consequence, if I weren't praised, I would think I had failed. I was constantly seeking approval and trying to please everyone. It was exhausting! Furthermore, it gave others the power to intimidate or manipulate me by withholding praise.

•   I felt different than anyone else. Even though I was an honor student, and involved in every possible activity at school and church, I felt as though I were on the outside looking in, with no one to confide in.

The condition of my heart back then reminds me of one of the teacups that my Russian friend Tanya brought me when she visited our home in the U.S. a few years ago. In the course of the long journey here, it had become cracked.

Tanya was devastated, so my husband immediately set about fixing it with strong, clear glue. After the glue dried, the teacup *looked* fine, but it had lost its *integrity*. It was no longer consistently true, through and through. And if it were bumped in the same place again, it would have quickly fallen apart. If only we could have restored it to its original condition with no hidden weaknesses!

Without Wax

Integrity is an interesting word. The ancient Greeks and Romans defined it as: Soundness; without wax.

To understand that, think about the pillars in their grand public buildings. Remember the three kinds of pillar design—Ionic, Doric, and Corinthian?

The story goes that when the surface of those pillars became chipped or weather beaten, the ancients had an interesting plan to deal with the problem. They hid the imperfections by filling the cracks with wax. But on particularly hot days, what would happen? The wax would melt.

Our Condition

We're like those pillars. Throughout our lives, we receive bruises and wounds and do embarrassing things. We sin and are sinned against, and we feel battle scarred. But because we don't want anyone to know how hurt or angry we feel inside, we try to fix ourselves. We patch. We cover over our wounds and sins by trying harder to please others and gain their approval, or by building a hard shell around our hearts while putting on a happy face.

But when the heat is turned up, what happens? The wax melts. Under the pressures of life, our protective devices fail. Every crack is exposed, and all our flaws show. Unfortunately, the temptation is always there to patch again when the temperature goes down. However, if we merely patch, the stress will never end.

Integrity Lost

Think again about what chips away at our spirits and destroys our wholeness or integrity:

- Sinful things we do. These usually produce guilt and shame, and then it's hard to forgive ourselves. We try to make amends by beating ourselves up over it, but only feel worse. We can't imagine that God could possibly forgive us.

- Sinful things others do to us. Sometimes we even believe that we somehow deserved it, when we didn't. We respond by either thinking we are worthless or by taking revenge through refusing to forgive. The lies we believe at these times often shape how we then relate to God. We think: "God, you weren't there for me. I must harden my heart to protect myself, because you won't help me."

- Simply being in a sinful world. We sometimes get caught in the crossfire of others' sinful choices and behavior. It's not God's fault, but we blame Him.

I realized how powerful this last one is by the reaction of a certain woman at a conference I was conducting in India a few years ago. At one point in the conference, I was addressing the issue of "free will" given to all people by God. I shared the illustration of how a bus driver could choose by his free will to be drunk and then cause an accident that would harm innocent men, women, and children.

Was that God's fault? Did He condone such behavior? Was He oblivious to the victims' suffering? No. It broke His heart! The harm that came to those people was a result of their being caught in the middle of the choices that the driver had made before he ever got on that bus. And for those choices, the driver would be responsible before a just God.

One of the women began crying. You see, someone had broken into her home several years before and shot her husband, killing him for no other reason than that the gunman was drunk. As I was teaching, God had revealed to this precious woman that her husband's murder had broken *His* heart as well and that He was grieving with her.

She realized in that moment that she had blamed God for her husband's death, as though He hadn't cared. She immediately asked God to forgive her for her anger at Him and let the anger flow to the Cross. And the bitterness in her heart melted away. Finally, joy was a possibility in her life.

Looking Inward

How do we know when there is a problem in *our* lives? Luke 6:43, 44 tells us that we can tell a tree by its fruit.

No good tree bears bad fruit, nor does a bad tree bear good fruit. Each tree is recognized by its own fruit. (NIV)

When we become believers in Jesus Christ, God sends a deep taproot down into the center of our lives as He establishes His presence there in the form of His Holy Spirit. However, even though we become alive to Him and sensitive to His presence, many old patterns of behavior, rooted in what we have experienced or believed in the past, still try to control us. While many unhealthy patterns, habits and beliefs were dislodged when we accepted Jesus as our Savior, others must be consciously dealt with as they are revealed to us now.

Our Healing

Jesus comes to us with compassion and deep understanding of our sin and suffering. As we invite Him to heal us, He reaches down into the tangled roots of our lives and gently leads us out of the pain. He reveals to us His love and mercy, and our hearts respond. As we repent and forgive, He breaks the power of past sins and wounds and heals our broken hearts. He offers us simple, profound secrets that will keep us free as we face the surprises and hardships of life.

These secrets are found in Scriptures. Consider how they apply to your life.

• Matthew 6:14 tells us that we must let go of our resentments of others and forgive before we can fully experience the forgiveness and fresh start that God offers when we ask Him to forgive *us*.

• Matthew 7:1-2 and Luke 6:37 tell us not to judge others harshly, condemning them and demanding restitution. He warns us that we are inviting disaster into our own lives when our hearts are hard toward others.

• Exodus 20:12 and Proverbs 20:20 stress how important it is to honor our parents (recognize and appreciate the great value they are to God) so that life will go well for us. We are warned that if we curse our parents, our spiritual insight will be darkened and we will not be able to see situations clearly. That does not mean that we excuse every bad thing they did, but it means that we leave their discipline and judgment up to God. We can simply show them respect as people for whom Christ died, just as He did for us.

- John 1:9 tells us that if we will confess and repent, God will freely forgive us and make our hearts clean again.

- Galatians 6:7 warns us that whatever we sow—whether blessing or cursing—will flow back into our own lives. We will reap what we sow. God set this law in motion in order to bless us when we treat others well. However, if we do evil to others, evil will likewise come back to us through others.

- Hebrews 12:15 stresses the importance of loving others—never letting offenses fester into bitterness which will spread its poison into every life we touch.

Applying His Love

It takes courage to face the evil, pain, and sorrow within our hearts and take it all to Jesus. It takes courage to give up revenge and forgive. It even takes courage, after many failures, to forgive and accept ourselves as God does. But on this journey, we will encounter *Him*, and that will make all the difference.

Can you imagine what it must have been like to be the woman caught in adultery, whose story is told in the eighth chapter of John? When she was dragged before the religious men to be stoned, the men challenged Jesus to join them in punishing her.

Instead of joining them, Jesus stooped to write something in the sand. I don't know what He wrote—maybe the Law of Moses in Leviticus 20:10 that demanded that *both* partners caught in adultery be punished. (Religious leaders had long before abandoned application of the Law equally to men and women). Or maybe He was making a list of the sins He knew *those men* had committed!

When he wrote in the dirt the second time, *maybe* He was writing a loving note of forgiveness and encouragement to the woman.

What I *do* know, however, is that He didn't look at her in disgust, nor did he humiliate or condemn her. He cared only that she be free of her shame and be given a new destiny, free of the past. Her sins were forgiven, her accusers dismissed as nothing, and she was sent on her way having been given a new start at life. The Law no longer had the power to bind her to her past sin, nor did those men.

She had an experience with the Son of God. In that experience, Jesus revealed the true character of His Father and His love for her. Her journey to joy had begun!

A Fresh Start

I love these verses in the Message Translation: *Now we look inside, and what we see is that anyone united with the Messiah gets a fresh start, is created new. The old life is gone; a new life burgeons! Look at it! All this comes from the God who settled the relationship between us and him, and then called us to settle our relationships with each other.* (2 Corinthians 5:17-19)

Remember: When Jesus touches our lives, He doesn't patch, He heals our hearts. As we are healed, a beautiful design emerges for all to see. God transforms the horrors of our pasts into a story of redeeming love. In the process, we are changed from the inside out.

The Bible says that we are transformed as God writes His laws of love on our hearts.

"This new plan I'm making with Israel isn't going to be written on paper, isn't going to be chiseled in stone; This time I'm writing out the plan in them, carving it on the lining of their hearts...they'll get to know me by being kindly forgiven, with the slate of their sins forever wiped clean." (Hebrews 8:10-12, quoting the Prophet Isaiah)

In His presence, as we repent and forgive, the pain is transformed into an experience that restores our integrity, making us whole again. We begin to understand the on-going process of being made new creatures—restored to His original intention for our lives. We will find our true selves perhaps for the first time!

Filled With New Life

I also love the way Jesus related to the Samaritan woman at the well (John 4). He brought transparency first, getting her to face her emptiness. Then He ministered to her real need: to be loved with a love that would never fail.

He told her He could give her *living* water—a relationship with Him that would completely satisfy her thirst. That's the revelation that changed her heart and set her on her own journey to joy!

Just as Jesus brought hope to her life, He can bring hope to ours. Jesus can not only create a beautiful story out of our lives, but He can fill us with living water—a refreshing, fulfilling relationship with Him. And when others look at us, they will no longer see our emptiness and thirst, but they will see the peace and joy that only Jesus can bring!

If God is speaking hope into your heart right now, pray this prayer with me right where you are:

"I surrender my sins and my wounds to you, Lord. I forgive those who have sinned against me (name them), and I cease seeking revenge through anger or by withholding love. I repent of the bitter root judgments I have made against you and others and ask you to break the control those judgments have had over my behavior. I want to be completely free to love others and to discover who I am in you!

"Lord, fill me with your life and your presence in a fresh and powerful way. Draw me to your side daily. Be Lord of every area of my life. No longer will I hide from you and others. Father, teach me how to honor you with great love and faithfulness. May I be a blessing to all who know me.

"Thank you for the miracle of a heart that has been set free! Show me how to carry your life with genuine love, transparency and joy. In Jesus' name, amen."

Chapter Two

Freed by the Truth

The next step on our journey to becoming who we were created to be is to break free of the lies we have believed about God, ourselves, and others.

To understand where these lies come from, let's go back to the beginning of the human race and the story of the fall of Adam and Eve in the Garden of Eden (Genesis 3). Satan tempted Eve to eat of the fruit by intimating that God was withholding something wonderful from her. He twisted truth and injected lying inferences. God took swift action against Satan and prophesied that someday Eve's seed (Jesus) would defeat Satan.

That old serpent has been at war against us ever since—in every generation and in every culture. He lies to us, enticing us to sin by making us doubt God's love. His tactics have changed very little through the centuries. His favorite is to whisper into our hearts horrible lies that minimize God's love and magnify our fears. He tries to get us to doubt God's integrity or suspect that somehow He is withholding good things from us. If we believe what Satan whispers, we may return to the insecurities, anger, and unforgiveness from which Jesus once set us free.

So how does this work in our lives? What makes us so gullible?

The Power of Lies

Recently, a young man named Cory shared with me a lie that had been controlling him for many years. He said sadly, "If I am ever to succeed, I must do it myself. I cannot trust anyone else to do what is best for me."

How did this lie gain entrance into Cory's belief system? It was planted in his heart when he was a teenager. In a fit of rage, his alcoholic father had thrown him out of the house and shouted, "You're on your own, kid! Don't come crying to me for help, because you won't get it!"

His father was thereafter unwilling to help or protect his son in the struggles of life. Consequently, as an adult, Cory was fiercely independent. It was difficult to trust others' motives or leadership. It was hard to stay at one job long enough to succeed. Since he expected to be let down or disappointed, he sometimes quit before his fears could be realized.

Mary, another friend of mine, recounted to me what her life has been like. "My mother committed suicide when I was eight years old.

A profound sense of being alone and vulnerable gripped me at the time. Something told me, 'You will always be alone. No one will care for you or protect you. That's just the way it is.'" As a result, Mary has never invested in friendships or marriage. She has spent the best years of her life alone, overwhelmed by a sense of hopelessness.

Still another friend, Jennifer, told me about how her father had sexually abused her. When her heart was bruised and her body violated, she grabbed hold of Satan's lie, "No man can be trusted." Because of believing this lie, she has been unable to trust her husband no matter *how* faithful he is. Her constant suspiciousness is driving him away.

Satan often takes advantage of our vulnerability during traumatic experiences to sow lies into our lives. We believe the lies at the time because we think doing so will protect us from such things happening again. But instead of protecting us from future evil, they usually make us a magnet for more evil.

These lies also isolate us from others who could help us, and distort our view of our heavenly father. Life becomes a constant struggle. Soon our expectations of doom become self-fulfilling prophecies.

My Own Lie

For several years, I had two very vivid, recurring and unsettling dreams about high school and college. In high school, my class was very small. Its members fell into two distinct groups, with little in between: the party crowd and the very studious college prep crowd. I didn't fit into either group. I didn't drink, so I didn't fit in with the party crowd whose fun usually included alcohol. I was an honor student, but I dated and was involved in many extra-curricular activities, so I didn't really fit in with the college prep group who focused almost exclusively on their studies.

The dream about high school was this: I walked into the school lunchroom with my tray of food and headed for an empty seat with the studious crowd. However, as I attempted to sit down, one of the girls turned to me with a smug smile and said, "We're saving this seat for someone else." Then when I turned toward the table of partiers, they just looked at me and laughed! So, in the dream, I sat alone.

The other dream was similar and came out of insecurities I experienced at the first college I attended. I dreamed that whenever I went into the Student Union to relax, there was absolutely no one who welcomed me into their group. Everyone was laughing and having a good time, while I just stood at the door alone.

I asked God to explain these dreams to me. He revealed to me that they were rooted in a lie that I had believed when I was a teenager. The lie was: "You are odd, and you will never fit in."

Redeeming Purpose

I began to see that God has sent those dreams to bring the lie to the surface so that I could be free of it. When I realized this, I went back, in my heart, to those days and forgave each person whom I had thought hadn't wanted me around. I asked Jesus to forgive me for believing that I was unwanted and odd, and I thanked Him for loving me.

Then I asked God to bless each of those who I had thought had rejected me.

That very night, I dreamed again. Only this time, when I walked into the high school lunchroom with my tray of food and headed toward the empty chair, the very girl who had smugly turned me away before waved me to the seat with a big smile of welcome. That dream was followed by another: When I entered the college Student Union, everyone turned to greet me with a smile and invited me to join them! When I woke up, I knew I was free.

God revealed to me two truths about the situation: **He** *had always wanted and loved me, and that it was **all right** to be different!* Being different didn't mean that I was unwanted or inferior. The judgment that I had felt wasn't from those students in high school or college, it was from the enemy who had distorted my memories because he wanted to steal my joy and isolate me from others.

Satan's ultimate plan had been to make me feel so insecure that I would give up the call to follow God on the uncharted, unusual course of taking the message of His healing and redemption to men and women around the world. But Satan's plan didn't work! God set me free by revealing how *He* felt about me and the *truth* about myself.

Isn't it amazing how intent the enemy is on trying to steal our confidence and destinies?

Lies We Commonly Believe

I recently asked both women and men at my church to describe the lies that Satan whispers to them regularly. Here is what they told me:

What Satan Tells Women:

- You are worthless and insignificant.
- You are not smart enough or spiritual enough to be of any great value to God.
- Your dreams are not important to Him. You'd fail at fulfilling them anyway.
- Others are dissatisfied with you.
- Your past sins and mistakes will haunt you forever.
- Others can be forgiven, but not you.
- You are so incredibly stupid! Why would anyone want to be your friend?
- Men are the world changers, not you. If you speak up for justice, you are pushy or too aggressive.
- Since you are a daughter of Eve, you are more easily deceived than men. Therefore, you can't be trusted with leadership.
- It is *your* fault if a man looks at you lustfully.
- You are not pretty enough, thin enough, or smart enough to be loved and respected by others.

- Life is just too hard. If you end your life, no one will miss you.

What Satan Tells Men:
- You're worthless.
- You can't trust God or anyone else to help you achieve success.
- You're a failure if you're not wealthy or have a highly-valued position or education.
- If you share your feelings, you're weak.
- Men should never cry.
- You must act tough if you want to be a real man.
- You are a disappointment to God.

What Satan Tells Women with Families:
- You are responsible for everyone in your family. Everything rests on your shoulders.
- If your children get into trouble, it's because you have failed as a mother.
- If your husband is unhappy, it's because you haven't done enough to please him.
- If you only had a more considerate husband, your life would be worth living.

What Satan Tells Husbands:
- You must have all the answers and solve all the problems; after all, you're the man.
- If you seek a woman's counsel, she will take advantage of you.
- You must make sure you are the one in control.

What Satan Tells Singles:
- You are only half a person without a romantic relationship.
- God's love is definitely not enough to make you happy or fulfilled.
- God has forgotten you.
- You are a misfit in a couple's world.
- You can't minister effectively as a single woman.
- If you don't experience childbirth, you're not a real woman.
- The reason no one wants to marry you is because you're not good enough.

The Danger

If we believe any of these lies, we'll do one or more of the following:
- We will doubt God's love and goodness.
- We will try to hide our feelings of hopelessness by keeping others at a distance.
- We will stuff our pain under good works, trying to be of value.
- We will try desperately to belong somewhere and lose our identity in the process.
- We will become depressed or angry or stuff ourselves with food, alcohol, or drugs.
- We will never pursue our God-given dreams.

Do you realize what a malicious enemy Satan is? John 8:44 tells us that *the devil was a murderer from the beginning, not holding to the truth, for there is no truth in him. When he lies, he speaks his native language, for he is a liar and the father of lies!*

Personally, I'm tired of the beating we take from Satan, but also the beating we give ourselves and each other because of the lies we have believed!

My heart is broken over men and women who feel betrayed or abandoned and whose lives are swallowed up in grief over losses, or who become tough and defensive. I'm shocked at how often we fall for Satan's lies and doubt God's good intentions, love and power.

Finding Freedom

Friends, Jesus is not only the Way and the Life, but also the *Truth* that sets us free! We must become men and women who go to His Word and believe Him for who we are. His Word is the two-edged sword that exposes the truth that sets us free.

So what does Scripture tell us that can set the record straight?

The Truth!

God loves me with an everlasting love. (Jeremiah 31:3)

Nothing can separate me from His amazing love! (Romans 8:35)

I am so loved by God that He gave His only Son to die so that I might live. (John 3:16)

I am His child, and I am wonderfully made. (Psalm 139:14)

He cherishes and honors me. (Isaiah 43:4)

He delights in me. He rejoices over me with singing! (Zephaniah 3:17)

He takes pleasure in me. (Psalm 149:4)

He is with me and thinks about me constantly. (Psalm 139:17-18)

He is for me, not against me. (Romans 8:31)

He revives me when I am weary. (Isaiah 40:31; Matthew 11:28; Psalm 62:5)

He takes my cares and gives me strength. (Psalm 55:22)

He is my strength and brings me joy. (Psalm 28:7)

I will become mature as I follow Him! (James 1:4)

He will give me success. (Joshua 1:7)

He has removed my sin as far as the east is from the west. (Psalm 105:12)

I am the righteousness of God in Christ Jesus! (2 Corinthians 5:21)

He heals my broken heart. (Psalm 34:18; Isaiah 53:5)

Jesus calls me His friend! (John 15:15)

I can walk in the same spiritual inheritance as any other believer—regardless of race, gender, or social status. (Galatians 3:26-28; Ephesians 1:18-21)

He will fulfill His plans for me! (Psalm 138:8)

His plans for me are for good, not for evil. (Jeremiah 29:11)

He fills me with His Holy Spirit. (Acts 2:17-18)

He gives me spiritual gifts to use in ministry. (Romans 12:6-8; 1 Corinthians 12:7-11)

He will reward me for my labor. (Jeremiah 31:16)

He gives me authority over Satan and his demons. (Ephesians 6:10-13)

I am more than a conqueror through Jesus who loves me. (Romans 8:37)
I no longer need to fear death. (Hebrews 2:14-15)
Christ in me is my hope of glory! (Colossians 1:27)

And now, Jesus Christ is inviting you to believe Him, follow Him, and find freedom and victory. Go with Him all the way! No more second-guessing God's love, and no more hesitation or fear.

Pray with me:
"Father, I confess that I have believed the lie that _____

_____

_____

_____

_____ (fill in the blank). You have shown me that the truth is that

_____

_____

_____

____. Forgive me and establish the truth in my heart.

"As I speak the truth aloud whenever I hear the lies, use the truth to break the power of those lies in my life. Set me free! In Jesus' name, amen."

Chapter Three

Alive for a Purpose

On our journey with Jesus, our hearts are being healed and the lies we have believed are being destroyed. Now, He wants to give us hope for the future!

There's an interesting story in Joshua 3-5. The new generation of Hebrew wilderness wanderers had crossed over the Jordan River and set up camp. There, a purification and sanctification process began as the males were marked by circumcision of the flesh. Their new identity as a free people was established. Then they waited there for healing and for strength for the battles ahead. Finally, they arose and began taking literal possession of the Promised Land.

Our own journey likewise involves crossing "the Jordan" when we experience new birth—a miracle, a fresh start. This is followed by the circumcision of our hearts as pride, shame, and selfishness are cut away and our new identities are established. Next, comes the healing and restoration that many of us have been experiencing. And finally, we are ready to fulfill the purpose for which we were born.

Since the fall in the Garden of Eden, we have struggled to know what we were created for. This side of the Cross, we begin the search by first receiving ourselves as fully as Jesus Christ receives us. As we find our identity in Him, we regain our capacity to live out our life purpose. We do it by His strength in us.

Dreamers

Jesus has always been a dreamer. One of His dreams has been that we become one with Him and one with each other. After praying for those who had come to faith under His immediate ministry, He prayed for us:

I'm praying not only for them but also for those who will believe in me because of them and their witness about me. The goal is for all of them to become one heart and mind—just as you, Father, are in me and I in you. So they might be one heart and mind with us. Then the world might believe that you, in fact, sent me. The same glory you gave me, I gave them, so they'll be as unified and together as we are—I in them and you in me. Then they'll be mature in this oneness, and give the godless world evidence that you've sent me and loved them in the same way you've loved me. John 17:20-23 (The Message)

May His dream become a reality!

While I was in college, I saw another dreamer on the evening news night after night. Martin Luther King had a dream that someday people would not be judged by the color of their skin, but by the content of their character. Dr. King's speeches struck a chord deep within my heart. His dream launched a cultural revolution in this country that continues today.

Now, I too am a dreamer. My dream is that someday there will be a "Symphony" playing for the Maestro. In this metaphorical symphony, men and women will serve God side by side without thought to gender or position. Together, we will reflect order and unity; mutual respect and diversity; and obedience to the Holy Spirit's score. The music (ministry) we will produce will glorify God alone.

What qualifies a person to be called a true dreamer (not a day dreamer)?

I believe that a dreamer:

- *Sees the sin, injustice or need*
- *Feels the pain with those who suffer*
- *Knows that there is a better way*
- *Has a biblical plan*
- *Is willing die for the dream if necessary*

Birth of the Dream

How did my dream of the "Symphony" begin? In 1996, I was invited by Dr. Joseph Umidi, Divinity Professor at Regent University in Virginia Beach, and Kevin Hinman, Founder of Leadership Training International, to team up with them to hold a leadership training conference for a gathering of about 225 emerging church leaders in Murmansk, Russia.

I had expected to play a minor role because I was a woman, but I was assigned as many seminar tracks as the men and given respect by them publicly as a full teammate.

Furthermore, the Russian pastor who was our host expected me to take my turn preaching to the public in the evening, and it was on that trip that I preached my first sermon. To my amazement, the Holy Spirit moved through *my* sermon as well!

I came back totally changed in my perception of oneness in ministry. It was my first experience of Body ministry based on gifting and maturity rather than gender. It lit a fire of passion in my heart to see all men and women serving God side by side, respecting each other's gifts fully.

My dream of the symphony is battered and bruised at times, and I sometimes think churches will never get to such a place of mutual respect. But I can't give up. The dream comes from the heart of God and must be pursued.

When Times Are Hard

Maybe you have dreams that have taken a beating, also. But when you feel like giving up, read the eleventh chapter of Hebrews and be encouraged by the stories of all those who, down through the generations, paid the price to obey God's call on their lives and stand for a God-given cause. Many of them died before seeing their dreams fulfilled, and you may as well. But stay faithful to what God tells you to do, and keep true to your dreams just as they did. God may surprise you with what He *will* do in your lifetime!

You may say, "But I'm a *nobody!* How can I expect to make a difference in the world?" Or, "I'm just one person in a culture that doesn't value my dream or my gifts!" Well, there's a story in the Bible, set in ancient times, of a woman who lived in a very patriarchal culture who was used by God powerfully to change history for Israel. Her name was Deborah.

An Unlikely Leader

Deborah is one of my heroes. At a time when the nation of Israel had strayed far from the worship of Jehovah and had been taken into captivity by the Canaanites, God raised up a woman as a prophet and judge over the nation. Over the period of Deborah's rule, Israel gained her freedom as this courageous woman made wise decisions and led them into battle. What was the result? The entire land had peace for forty years.

What I love best about her story is that she always knew that it was God who gave her wisdom and brought the victories. She just needed to be obedient. Furthermore, rather than taking credit for her role in those victories, she gave credit to God and praised others for their courage. She fulfilled her destiny because she followed God with faith and confidence.

If you still think God can't use you today, consider the prophecy in Joel 2:28-29 that Peter declared was being fulfilled at Pentecost: *"In the last days, God said, I will pour out my Spirit upon all people. Your sons and daughters will prophesy, your young men will see visions, and your old men will dream dreams. In those days I will pour out my Spirit upon all my servants, men and women alike, and they will prophesy..."* We are *all* needed to share the Gospel and bring hope to this dark world. The Holy Spirit will empower us if we invite Him to fill us and use us.

Becoming Like Jesus

The heart of Paul's message to us in the Bible is his plea that we all—men and women alike—grow up to be like Christ and make His ways known. This can change the world—one life, one family, one community, one nation at a time. We have all been given spiritual gifts and abilities we are responsible to use. As we obey and trust God, His power and authority will be released through us to bring hope to a desperate world.

To be like Jesus will require putting God's will first. This will mean having pure and forgiving hearts, being authentic and compassionate, and being willing to pay any price to fulfill the dream.

However, in the pursuit of God's plan for our lives—especially when success is the closest—Satan will always attack us with feelings of unworthiness and try to get us to give up. During such attacks, we can learn to look into the shadows of the worst we have been and then beyond that to the cross of Christ. At the cross, we will see His blood shed for us. There, we will find that we are in love with Him, and He with us. That love is more desperate and deeply rooted than we could ever imagine it could be.

Out of our love affair with Jesus will flow the fulfillment of His purpose for our lives.

Get Ready

God asks you and me to be outrageously convinced that the purpose of our time here on earth is truly significant...so convinced that we will not give up the pursuit of the spiritual dreams He has placed in our hearts.

How about you? Are you outrageously convinced?

What have you been called to champion? Do you have a clear vision?

God gives an important directive that speaks to us today regarding our holy dreams: *Write down the revelation and make it plain on tablets so that a herald may run with it. For the revelation awaits an appointed time; it speaks of the end and will not prove false. Though it linger, wait for it; it will certainly come and will not delay.* Habakkuk 2: 2-3 (NIV)

If God is giving you a dream for your life, write the vision down, and write it plainly so you can run with it. Describe it. *You'll never do what you cannot visualize.*

Then let God calculate the route and adjust the timing. When He says to move, step out by faith and continue until you reach your destination. Throughout the journey, align yourself with others who are also pursuing God's plan for their lives and will encourage you.

Be Strong

The world is a frightening mess, I know! It may take a very long time to see our dreams fulfilled. We will need His power, guidance and protection. But listen to what Paul says in Ephesians 6:12-18:

And that about wraps it up. God is strong, and he wants you strong. So take everything the Master has set out for you, well-made weapons of the best materials. And put them to use so you will be able to stand up to everything the Devil throws your way. This is no afternoon athletic contest that we'll walk away from and forget about in a couple of hours. This is for keeps, a life-or-death fight to the finish against the Devil and all his angels.

Be prepared. You're up against far more than you can handle on your own. Take all the help you can get, every weapon God has issued, so that when it's all over but the shouting you'll still be on your feet. Truth, righteousness, peace, faith, and salvation are more than words. Learn how to apply them. You'll need them throughout your life. God's Word is an indispensable weapon. In the same way, prayer is essential in the on-going warfare. Pray hard and long. Pray for your brothers and sisters. Keep your eyes open. Keep each other's spirits up so that no one falls behind or drops out. (The Message)

And stay on your knees. Frances Frangipane once said: "Satan is terrified of humility; he hates it. He sees a humble person and it sends chills down his back. His hair stands up when Christians kneel down, for humility is the surrender of the soul to God. The devil trembles before the meek because in the very areas where he once had access, there stands the Lord!"

Don't Quit

Finally, be encouraged by reviewing the price those who went before us in the faith were willing to pay:

Do you see what this means—all these pioneers who blazed the way, all these veterans cheering us on? It means we'd better get on with it. Strip down, start running—and never quit! No extra spiritual fat, no parasitic sins. Keep your eyes on Jesus, who both began and finished this race we're in. Study how he did it. Because he never lost sight of where he was headed—that exhilarating finish in and with God—he could put up with anything along the way: cross, shame, whatever. And now he's there, in the place of honor, right alongside God. When you find yourselves flagging in your faith, go over that story again, item by item, that long litany of hostility he plowed through. That will shoot adrenaline into your souls! Hebrews 12:1-3 (The Message)

Please pray with me:

"Light a fire of passion in my heart, Lord. Cause me to love what you love and hate what you hate, and be courageous in doing something about it. Most of all, move me to profoundly care that the lost and wounded come to know that you love them. Transform my pain into compassion.

"Give me big dreams! Then give me the ability to run my race with dignity, passion, and grace. As your beloved child and heir of your kingdom, I claim my position in you and commit myself to bring you glory.

"Thank you for invading my life with your love and purpose. I will never be the same.
I praise you, Lord God, for giving me a wonderful future. In Jesus' name, amen!"

If God is giving you a dream that He wants you to pursue for His glory, write it clearly below:

_____
_____
_____
_____
_____
_____
_____

Part 2

Learning to Love

Chapter Four

Resisting the Assault on Purity

My dear friend Lori is alone again after twenty years of marriage. Her husband, who had been addicted to pornography since he was a teenager, had an affair with another woman. When discovered, he was unwilling to break off the relationship with that woman. Instead, he divorced Lori.

Lori loves God very much, but she struggles occasionally with her resolve to remain sexually pure in the future as a single woman. Having been married for so long, she wonders if, since her virginity is far behind her, it may not matter what she does now. But in her heart, she knows that purity (having sex only within the covenant of marriage) is still important to God, and she wants to please Him.

Not long ago, I received this email from her:

Dear Joyce,

Please tell me clearly why the Lord wants us to wait for marriage to have sex. What are the good reasons? Please don't be alarmed that I am asking this. I am not planning anything. I just want to hear His encouragement, and I know you'll have the right words for me. Please take a moment and write to me.

Love, Lori

Dear Lori,

I'll keep this very simple and share what has made sense to me. It all goes back to three things: our preciousness to God as carriers of His image; His intention for sex to accompany a lasting oneness within marriage; and the sacredness of our bodies.

In the Message translation, 1 Corinthians 6 speaks most clearly to this issue. Verses 13-20 read like this:

"God honored the Master's body by raising it from the grave. He'll treat yours with the same resurrection power. Until that time, remember that your bodies are created with the same dignity as the Master's body. You wouldn't take the Master's body off to a whorehouse, would you (meaning to have sex for its own sake without the commitment of marriage and faithfulness)? I should hope not. There's more to sex than mere skin on skin. Sex is as much spiritual mystery as physical fact. As written in Scripture, "the two become one." Since we want to become spiritually one with the Master, we must not pursue the kind of sex that avoids commitment and intimacy, leaving us more

lonely than ever—the kind of sex that can never 'become one.'

"There is a sense in which sexual sins are different from all others. In sexual sin we violate the sacredness of our own bodies, these bodies that were made for God-given and God-modeled love, for 'becoming one' with another. Or didn't you realize that your body is a sacred place, the place of the Holy Spirit? Don't you see that you can't live however you please, squandering what God paid such a high price for? The physical part of you is not some piece of property belonging to the spiritual part of you. God owns the whole works. So let people see God in and through your body."

Lori, you first and foremost belong to God— every single part of you. Whatever you bring into that relationship either blesses or grieves Him. He lives your experiences with you. His blessing is on sex within marriage, and He grieves over the selfish use of a wonderful gift when sex is indulged in outside of marriage.

As you know, God hates divorce because of the violence it does to our spirits when they are torn apart (Malachi 2:13-16). He doesn't want us to suffer. He hates sexual promiscuity for the same reason. The loneliness that follows casual sex, and the devaluing that it promotes, can be overwhelming even to those who don't know God.

Thank God for the cross and the forgiveness for our past behavior! The slate is wiped clean. But how horrible it is to treat His suffering for our sins as incidental or of little consequence—which we do when we act as though keeping our bodies pure for Him *doesn't matter. I thank God that you understand this, dear friend!*

Much love, Joyce

To which she responded:

Thank you so very much for your thoughts, Joyce. I was meditating on them last night. Truly, I know what is right in my heart...but I have never been challenged about sex outside marriage until this time in my life.

Just thinking about it the way you presented it—reminding me of how precious my body is, how it belongs to the Lord, how He suffered in HIS body for me to give me forgiveness and freedom from sin—is powerful. It has been awhile since I considered it with these things in mind. When I think of His deep and tender love for me, I ask myself, "How could I hurt Him Who loves me so? How could I not do what He asks of me?" But it goes even deeper to remember his suffering for me.

*Joyce, even Christians seem to forget these truths. In my conversations with single Christian women, I find many who hardly hesitate to have sex with a man if they have strong feelings toward him. I have even been encouraged to "Go ahead! If God doesn't like it, He will forgive you." It must grieve the Lord so...I couldn't grieve Him so, because I know He is so in love with me. I **do not** want to do that. Oh! May He live in me to be strong and valiant and enable me to fulfill His commands of LOVE!*

*It is good for me, also, to remember that immorality is destructive to me. But I tell you, Joyce, this culture is so deafening when it comes to pressuring us to believe that it is acceptable, and even **healthy**, to engage in sin! And so, I thank you for* *taking the time to write me and remind me of these things.*

Love, Lori

There are millions of men and women like Lori who are struggling to know what is right. Maybe you are one of them.

We all know that our deepest needs have not changed, no matter what we have gone through. We long for the true love that is marked by faithfulness, purity, innocence and respect. However, we are tempted to forget that *marriage* is the commitment of true love, and sex is the *fulfillment* of that marriage commitment.

But how can we resist sex before marriage when our culture proposes that it's our natural "right"? How did we get to this view?

Tracing Our Current Confusion

The pressures are great all over the world to deny the existence or value of moral absolutes. Furthermore, there has been a major shift away from recognizing and valuing the intrinsic worth of the individual before God.

Much has changed within my own lifetime. When I was in college during the '60s, everything past generations had ever believed was up for scrutiny on a scale never before seen in the United States. Morality, faithfulness, and the sanctity of marriage and of life itself—even the existence of God—were in question. We were terribly naïve and, at the same time, incredibly arrogant.

In the shadows of the Viet Nam War, a war that grew more senseless by the day—my generation began to create a new reality. "Why work toward a tomorrow that may never come? Why follow our parents' morality while the leaders from their generation play chess with our lives? Why not 'love' freely on impulse? After all, life is short."

At the same time, the theory of evolution was gaining support. This theory—that we were simply a higher form of animal life rather than created by God in His image—had a grave effect on us. It seemed to release us from God-honoring civility and self- restraint. If animals could behave instinctively, why couldn't we? Being responsible for our behavior to a holy God gradually became an archaic concept to many young people.

Furthermore, existentialism—which espoused self-actualization as man's highest goal—had reached America. The German philosopher Nietzche's contention, "God is dead," deepened the fear that we were, indeed, alone. It followed, then, that we weren't accountable to anyone but ourselves. Soon, public schools began teaching "situation ethics" to our young people. A general self-centeredness emerged from this disregard of God and moral absolutes. Few in our generation read and understood Psalm 52:1 which states: *The fool says in his heart, "There is no God."*

Today, we realize that what "free love" (sex outside marriage) and these philosophies have done to us, especially women, is to make us *common*. Sex and the human body have lost their preciousness, becoming sources of entertainment or commodities to be consumed.

The consequences of our self-centeredness continue. Divorce because of sexual unfaithfulness is decimating our families, creating enormous loneliness, and generating anger among the children of divorced parents.

Many young men, raised in fatherless homes with few or no reliable male role models, are at a loss as to how to faithfully provide for their families and honor women. In the worst cases, they are fathering children at will and then abandoning them. In the U.S., 33% of our young women between the ages of 15 and 20 become pregnant while single.

There is also an alarming trend among teenage boys to treat their girlfriends in demeaning ways. On the *Today Show* recently, an authority on teen behavior said that one-fifth of all girls are abused by their boyfriends. Because girls from broken homes are as insecure as the boys and at a loss as to how to relate in healthy ways to the opposite sex, they feel powerless to stop the cycle of abuse. They often feel that they deserve the mistreatment. Their fathers had abandoned them, so they wonder if they are not, after all, unworthy of love and faithfulness.

Both sexes are reaching out for human touch and love. But the way in which they do it often flows out of anger, raw selfishness, or vast loneliness. They desperately need to know what *true* love is.

A Timeless Tale

There's a story in the Bible that breaks my heart every time I read it (2 Samuel 13). It's the tragic story of the beautiful young daughter of King David. By having several wives, King David had created a blended family. Within that family were step-brothers and sisters who, while legally related, were sexually tempting to one another.

David's son Amnon thought he was in love with his half-sister Tamar because his sexual desire for her was so strong. He desperately wanted to possess her. However, the king's virgin daughters were kept in seclusion, so Amnon couldn't get near her.

His friend Jonadab, a shrewd man, saw Amnon's frustration and suggested a plan to get the king to send Tamar to him. Amnon was to pretend to be sick and request to be fed by his sister. David fell for the ruse and sent Tamar to him.

Although Tamar tried desperately to resist him, Amnon overcame her physically and raped her. In a culture in which a woman's virginity was the key to a successful marriage and a secure future, Amnon had ruined her. And in the end, once Amnon had taken from her what he wanted, he despised her! What he had felt had never been love—only lust.

The Lesson

True love protects, honors, and cherishes the other person. True love waits to have sex within the safety and security of marriage.

But unlike Tamar, many of us, especially when we are young, don't resist sexual advances.

We actually invite them. We naively think that if we have sex with our boyfriends, love and commitment will follow. The opposite is usually true. In the end, Tamar's fate is often ours. Rather than being treasured, we are treated with disdain, having become common. *One single friend of mine expressed her frustration with other single women—who are willing to have sex with every man they date—like this: "They are **training** the men to treat all women as common!"*

Even if we think we are in love and live together, without the commitment of marriage for life, there is less incentive to work at the relationship. When disagreements or adversity comes, one or the other of us can simply flee if the pressure seems overwhelming. Consequently, telling the truth usually seems too risky if we don't want the other to leave. Tolerating living together without being married often simply sustains unresolved relational dysfunction indefinitely.

Addictive Behaviors

Sex with several partners can not only brings disease, but often opens up a bottomless well of desire for more that is never filled or satisfied. For those who habitually access pornography, the chasm of unfulfilled desire deepens. The fascination and excitement—which draw them into viewing pornographic images and others' sexual behavior—turn into a demoralizing and dehumanizing addiction.

Repeated exposure to pornography basically de-socializes the users, slowly ruining them for authentic, healthy relationships. All thoughts are on themselves. Pursuing sex through viewing pornography teaches them nothing about how to be in relationship with people in the real world where there must be understanding, sensitivity, respect, communication, and self-control. Eventually, they may even lose their ability to function sexually within an authentic relationship.

Activities that are rooted in fantasy, such as viewing pornography, cause us to miss the treasure in the lives of those around us who are seeking to love us. Indeed, life becomes one-dimensional—physical only. Everyone starves emotionally and spiritually when trying to live on such a level.

The prophet Jeremiah understood this well. He wrote:

"My people have committed two sins: They have forsaken me, the spring of living water, and have dug their own cisterns, broken cisterns that cannot hold water. Consider then and realize how evil and bitter it is for you when you forsake the Lord your God and have no awe of me," declares the Lord, the Lord Almighty. (Jeremiah 2:13 and 19b)

An Age-old Battle

Satan is clever, and we are naive at best. The most efficient way he can wound the human race and break the heart of God is by inspiring sexual sin and perversion. It not only wounds our bodies, but our souls and spirits as well.

The writer of Ecclesiastes tells us that there is nothing new under the sun. The lies run deep. The ancient Greek philosophers taught that men and women were two-part beings, body and soul, and that what they did with their bodies wouldn't affect their souls. They believed that that could have sex with temple prostitutes and still worship the gods on holy days.

However, the Hebrews had it right. They believed that we were created in the image of God as *three integrated, inseparable parts: body, soul and spirit.* The Bible teaches that what is done with our bodies also affects our spirits and souls. And what wounds our souls or spirits affects our bodies, and so on. Any one part affects every other part. Understanding this truth can give us strength to resist compromise on our journey to wholeness and joy.

Broken Promises

The truth is, something profound happens during sex. An unconscious promise is made that, if unfulfilled, brings confusion to our spirits and frustration to our minds, wills and emotions. Even the writers of secular movies know this. In one that was popular a few years ago, the man and woman agree to a purely physical relationship that is non-binding. However, when he decides to have a similar relationship with another woman at the same time, the first woman breaks into a rage. In defense, the guy protests that he had made no promises to her. To this she screams, "Even if *you* didn't promise, *your body did!*"

Casual sex has consequences beyond the obvious. The unspoken promises are very real to us: that we will devote ourselves *exclusively to each other; that we will love one another unselfishly and cherish each other forever; that we will become one.* We somehow automatically *know* that's the way it should be. God has designed us to function beautifully within faithfulness and commitment to one person for life. When that promise is denied, we are confused, frustrated, and angry. We feel betrayed.

In the United States, many couples are living together, unmarried. They say they are testing their compatibility before marriage to prevent divorce. They lived through their parents' divorce and don't want to repeat the pain. However, counselors tell us that sex before marriage often creates more problems after marriage than it prevents.

Some couples fear that *the excitement* will be gone if they get married. But what exactly is this excitement? Could it merely be the thrill of having stolen something to which they have no right? Proverbs 9:17-18 says: *Stolen water is sweet; food eaten in secret is delicious! But little do they know that the dead are there...*(NIV) Is that what God wants for us? Is that what *we* really want?

The Effects of Sexual Sin

Since the fall of Adam and Eve, Satan has been singing a song of counterfeit love to us—a song, that if we learn to sing it with him, will leave us empty and violated.   Sexual sin is more deadly than we realize.

1.   It pierces to our spirits where the Holy Spirit dwells. It is unfaithfulness to God most of all. (Mal. 2:13-16).

2.   It despises life that is precious to God. (We are spiritual brothers and sisters. We are one another's keeper!   To encourage one another to sin is a terrible spiritual burden and one we do not want to bear. Mt. 18:6)

3. It creates a tearing apart each time we change partners.

4.   It has adverse effects on future relationships.

      a. Fear of unfaithfulness

      b. Lack of trust

      c. Guilt (secrecy)

      d. Habits which are hard to break (flirting; hungering for illegitimate attention)

5.   It can cause disease, unwanted pregnancies, and despair. (Four million teens in the U. S. contract sexually transmitted diseases annually, and suicide is the third leading cause of death.)

Why do We Persist in Sexual Sin?

The *reasons* we sin sexually, other than simple naïveté, often remain with us even after we make a commitment to stay pure. So to be truly set free, we need to recognize and deal with the reasons. They may be that:

1. We have an unusually deep craving for approval or affection.

2. We see ourselves as rescuers.

3. We want to escape a bad home situation.

4. We're afraid of commitment because of the horror of our parents' divorce.

5. We have sexual addictions.

6. We are trying to prove ourselves.

7. We are simply lonely.

The Remedy

We must first find our hope in God through a relationship with Jesus Christ. Only He can heal us and enable us to experience true joy. He will give us His complete approval and set us free from having to prove our value by submitting to someone else's selfish demands. He will also help us forgive our parents, so we don't repeat their mistakes. If we have become addicted to pornography, He will provide the support, counseling and accountability within the safety of Christian community that we need to break that addiction.

Jesus promises to be our constant companion against loneliness. A new hope and future will emerge. A new dignity will fill us as we value ourselves and live to honor our holy God. And if we have become wrongly involved with someone simply because we wanted to help them out of their sorrows or problems, we can let them go and trust God with that life. Only He can save that person for whom we care.

A Fresh Start

God calls us to value ourselves and one another highly as made in His image. Our greatest gift to others is to respect them and do nothing to bring guilt or shame into their lives. God's desire is that we stay pure and free from humiliation. He wants us to experience *true* love.

As we go to Jesus with our past sins, He will forgive us and enable us to hold to our new convictions. We will find a core of steel rising within our spirits as we live in sexual freedom— the freedom to remain pure and faithful. We will be as God created us to be: holy, worthy of respect, complete in Him, and at peace with life.

A *Plan*

If you are single and dating, clarify your motives, and don't date just for the sake of dating. Determine early to please God by refraining from sex before marriage, and resist the pressures of the culture.

Be ready to remain single if someone suitable does not come on the scene. Don't settle for someone who doesn't share your values in life simply in order to get married. And while you're waiting, develop non-romantic relationships. (You might end up marrying a friend!) Search out those known for their character qualities, rather than appearance.

Realize that marriage isn't a dream world. It is only as healthy as the individuals involved, so not only look for a person worth marrying, *be* a person worth marrying! Furthermore, invite objective feedback about your relationship from spiritual friends whom you trust. Give them permission to speak truth or caution into your life. Glean also from your own parents' wisdom and the lessons they learned, no matter how old you are.

While you are dating, beware of excessive touching. It is addictive, and when it is frequent, it reduces verbal communication. It may hinder your speaking the truth to your friend out of fear of losing the comforts of touching. Frequent touching also creates casualness toward sex.

I often tell young people to be sure to receive counseling for any personal problems before dating. Then focus on growing spiritually, working faithfully, pursuing career plans, honoring your family members, and cultivating an attitude of gratefulness for life. Be creative, learn new things, and have fun.

When you meet that special person, value their dreams. Don't be threatened by them or possessive of their time and attention. Give them space to breathe. Allow for other friends for both of you. Get to know their family early in the relationship. Observe how they treat their parents and siblings within the context of their home. They will likely treat you the same way eventually.

Know your value to God. Out of that security, you will be able to speak honestly, and listen without being defensive.

The Final Word

Above all else, guard your heart, for it is the wellspring of life. Put away perversity from your mouth; keep corrupt talk far from your lips. Let your eyes look straight ahead, fix your gaze directly before you. Make level paths for your feet and take only ways that are firm. Do not swerve to the right or the left; keep your foot from evil. (Proverbs 4:23-27)

May sexual purity begin with you and me. As we respond to God's love, we will be able to give *true love* to others.

If you have been committing sexual sin, please pray with me:

"God, I am sorry for not valuing my life and my body the way you do. Forgive me for being naive and selfish in my relationships with the opposite sex. Forgive me for looking to sex for acceptance or to earn love with no regard for the harm it does to both of us. Cleanse me—body, soul, and spirit—and restore my purity.

"Please reach into my life and show me the root causes of my behavior. As I forgive myself and those who have influenced me or even abused me, heal me and teach me how to trust you completely in this area of my life.

"I choose now to see myself and others as You do—as holy and worthy to be protected and honored. I choose this day to commit myself to sexual purity."

_____(Your name)

_____(Today's date)

In Jesus' name, amen."

If you have been able to stay sexually pure, thank God for it right now. Make the choice to continue on this path with His help. Declare that choice below:

"I choose now to see myself and others as You do—as holy and worthy to be protected and honored. I choose this day to commit myself to sexual purity."

_____(Your name)
_____(Today's date)

Chapter Five

In Search of True Love

True Love: "The commitment to care deeply for the other, to preserve, cherish, protect, and honor."

True love is indeed wonderful, and watching it grow within marriage is a beautiful illustration of our relationship with God Himself.

My husband Jim and I enjoy going to the mall on Saturday nights after church to relax over a Starbucks latte and "people watch". I am especially fascinated by watching teenagers who behave exactly as my peers and I did at their age: traveling in a pack of chattering girlfriends, we were consumed with our own images reflected in every store window we pass, so concerned about the way we looked, wondering if anyone would find us attractive. If we encountered a group of guys, we tried our best to look and act desirable, while all the time thinking only of ourselves. And the guys were doing the same thing.

Back then, all of us showed attention to the opposite sex primarily to get attention back! I don't think we really cared in the least about knowing or understanding the guys, or they us. We were all looking for someone to validate us.

We were definitely not thinking about the definition of love that is written at the beginning of this chapter!

Unfortunately, most of us unknowingly enter into marriage still seeking that validation. We say that we love the one we marry, but we have only begun the journey to esteeming them more highly than we do ourselves. And the same is true for them.

Worshiping Someone Else

There was a song made popular in the 1950's entitled, "Only You." One of the lines went like this, *Only you can make my dreams come true...* That song still seems so romantic. But it's dangerous! If Adam had been singing it that day in the Garden when Eve offered him the fruit, it would explain why he didn't knock it right out of her hand and declare, "There's no way you and I are going to sin against God by eating that thing!" Songs like "Only You" describe how easily our center for fulfillment can move off from God and onto a person. This is the beginning of misery.

The fact is that no human being will be able to give to us all we expect of them. They cannot solve all our problems and, if they are not believers, they cannot even help us overcome loneliness. Indeed, only God can relieve the loneliness we experience, especially if that person is not a devoted follower of Jesus Christ.

If we marry someone who doesn't know Jesus yet, deriving our own security, peace, and freedom from the Lord Jesus Christ will be all the more critical. If our trust is in Him and not circumstances, we will be able to continue to be authentic as we wait for our mate to become all God intended.

Conversely, just as no human being is capable of meeting our deepest needs, we cannot heal *their* wounds with our love. They need an encounter with God.

An Intense Setting

God designed marriage to be an intense setting in which we face what we are and learn to love unselfishly. It is an exciting pilgrimage from individual self-centeredness to Oneness. There is no greater joy than loving someone who unconditionally loves us and has committed before God and man to cherish us until the day we die. There is no greater excitement than facing the challenges of life with someone who will fight the battles by our side without giving up. There is no greater satisfaction than raising our children together to become emotionally healthy, secure, God-honoring, faithful-hearted adults who know their value to Him and their purpose in life.

God's Plan

Marriage is a blessing: It brings us great joy, but it also reveals areas in which we need to mature. An area in which I desperately needed to mature was in what I allowed to define me. In the early days of our marriage, I often allowed my husband's behavior toward me to define me to myself. He didn't know yet how to express his love easily, and in the absence of words, I began to feel devalued. In response, I would withdraw emotionally and secretly devalue *him*.

I remember sitting up in bed one night, looking over at my sleeping husband and muttering to no one in particular,

"And I gave up all my options in life to marry *him?*"

To which the Holy Spirit immediately responded, "And he gave up all *his* options in life to marry *you...*" That was the first time I remember being convicted of my own self-centeredness and how little I valued or understood *him*.

Have you been there? Are you there now?

At such times, we have choices to make: Will we shape our responses to our spouses based on their weaknesses or on their strengths? Will we search for those strengths? Will we stop nursing our hurts, realize our input to their lives can be valuable, and approach them respectfully with the problem? Maybe our spouses simply don't realize what we need and how badly we need it.

It's amazing, that after I forgave my husband of his offenses and repented of my judgments against him, a new freedom emerged in our relationship. I became more confident in voicing my feelings and more sensitive to the ways in which I was ignoring his needs. As our relationship grew on a new foundation of mutual respect and honest communication, it was as though I was discovering my true self *and* a new husband—one who, I realize now, had been there all the time!

The Truth

Years ago, a male friend of mine declared: "Joyce, all men are basically selfish, and it's selfishness that causes all our problems in marriage." But because I know my own heart, I must correct that by saying, "We are *all* basically selfish!" Every part of who we are, whether we are men or women, needs to learn how to give "true love."

Regardless of our maturity level, we enter marriage as two diamonds in the rough. The process of "becoming one" chisels away at the selfishness and stubborn character flaws that we acquired during childhood, even in the best of homes. We learn the grace of honoring, making healthy compromises, serving, protecting, refreshing one another, yielding for the other's sake, and seeing God fulfill His promises to us when we are faithful.

Let me give you one very strong warning: Whenever we are dissatisfied with our mates, whenever we think we deserve better—or listen to people who tell us we deserve better—Satan will send someone who looks just like what we wish our spouse would be. That person will treat us with great tenderness, and say all the right words to make us feel like the most delightful, fascinating person on earth. But I have learned that a person who shows romantic affection to us when we are married to someone else has only one goal, whether subconscious or intentional: to meet his or her own need. *There is never a pure goal in the heart of a person who seeks intimacy with someone else's spouse. That person will surely bring nothing but grief into our lives.*

If we succumb to such attention, we become caught in an ancient, deadly trap. We fall for the lie that this attention is worthy of our worship or our devotion, and it becomes an idol that can do nothing good for us. So beware! Wake up! Isaiah 44:20 says it so well: *(She or He) feeds on ashes, a deluded heart misleads (her or him); (she or he) cannot save (herself or himself), or say, "Is not this thing in my right hand a lie?"*

It is not love, but hate. It does not honor us or our covenant with God or the vows we have taken, and it will not protect us from the pain that comes from betraying God and our mates if we are married. It will drag us into the pit of unfaithfulness—*if only of the heart*—which is as dangerous that that of the body. And if it is not stopped, it *will* become sexual.

Dangerous Affairs of the Heart

Emotional or spiritual adultery—that illegal knitting of soul and spirit that happens when we share our hearts with one who isn't our spouse—destroys our lives inch by inch without our realizing it at first. *It may blind us and cripple our lives or marriages for years and years before being discovered.* In fact, it may never be discovered, but it robs us of any and all of the joy God intends for our marriages. Even if we are single, we must resist entrusting the deep things of our lives with, or giving emotional support to, a married man or woman.

Emotional or spiritual adultery can happen to well-meaning men and women who have unhealed issues in their lives. They have no intention of doing anything wrong. But before long, the addiction to that other person's affection grows so strong, they are willing to sacrifice everything to keep the relationship alive—even commit sexual sin, if that's what it takes to hang onto the emotional gratification they are receiving. *Satan deceives* them into thinking it is true love—while in reality, it is the basest, most dysfunctional affection on the face of the earth.

For a believer, it is first and foremost unfaithfulness to God. David knew this. In speaking to God after he had committed adultery with Bathsheba, David confessed: *Against you, you only, have I sinned and done what is evil in your sight...* Psalm 51:4 (NIV)

How did David sin against God? He judged God's love as insufficient. He broke his covenant with God in which he had promised to obey His commands and trust Him for his own happiness.

God has not guaranteed any of us that we will be loved by someone in the way we desire, but He *has* promised that *He* will love us perfectly. When we make an idol out of human love and seek it from a co-worker, friend, or a stranger at any cost, our greatest sin is against God! We are first and foremost in covenant with *Him*.

My Own Journey

Years ago, I experienced this illegal affair of the heart, and I then wrote about it in my first book, ***Lambs on the Ledge***. Because of the book, I have received calls from men and women all over the United States who have found themselves sucked into spiritual or emotional adultery. Some lost everything—families, homes, and ministries—before discovering that such "love" was false and based on a lie. Others learned in time and are working to rebuild their marriages on an honest foundation. Now that the deception has been broken through repentance, they are learning how precious their mates really are to God, and they do not want to cause them any more pain. Trust is slowly being rebuilt. Within that context, true love is growing.

I am in awe of how God has changed my marriage. He has given both of us new hearts as we have forgiven each other and repented of our own roles in past hurts. We now love each other deeply and are each other's best friend. We are each other's champion and cheerleader in all areas of life. More than anything, we want what is best for each other. My husband does everything he can to help me be all that I can be in Christ and fulfill the dreams God has given me. In turn, I do all I can to bring him honor and help him fulfill the dreams God has given him. We are *two whole individuals* who have become one healthy whole together in God. We are guided in decisions together by God. In fact, God speaks to both of us. It is not a matter of either of us being more important; *God* is the head of our relationship and our home.

On a daily basis, we are *both* responsible to God to grow spiritually, and we are *both* responsible to fulfill the purposes for which God has us together. *The scripture that guides us is Philippians 2:15: Do nothing out of selfish ambition or vain conceit, but in humility consider others better than yourselves.* Philippians 2:15 (NIV)

Gentle Reminders

In closing, let me remind you of five simple acts or attitudes that will protect you who are married from being self-centered:

1. *Listen to your spouse attentively.*

2. *Don't lecture. Give time for the Holy Spirit to speak to them.*

3. *Even when they fail, continue to show respect.*

4. *Respect yourself and speak truthfully.*

5. *Say you're sorry quickly when you offend.*

6. *Forgive before the day ends. Never go to bed angry.*

7. *Remember that this love is a gift from*

God. Thank Him for your spouse.

8. Share with each other both your emotional and your sexual needs and come to a mutually respectful way of meeting them together.

9. Pray together each day, even the simplest of prayers. It keeps life in perspective and it keeps you both honest.

Our Responsibility

Any marriage or friendship will be only as healthy as each individual is. We are responsible to come to God for ourselves, whether we are married or single, to grow into healthy reflections of His nature individually. As believers, we are partners in the faith and partners in life, meant to use our gifts together as a cohesive whole. When this is done in marriage and throughout the church, it is a perfect model of what the Body of Christ should be. Then together we will reflect God's nature to the next generation.

The key to healthy relationships is to first recognize others' great worth to God, then to invest in their lives by honoring them. As we remember the weaknesses in our own lives, we will find patience for the same in theirs.

If we honor others—see them as precious to God—we will not abuse them or lead them into sin. We will see them as individually precious to God and, therefore, individually precious to us.

For All of Us

My dream is that the level of mutual honoring of one another, especially in the church, will rise to a new high. Both married and single parents need to experience this mutual love and respect, and their children need to see them giving and receiving it. This will teach the children much about the character of God and instill a clear identity of worth within their hearts. It will also teach them how to behave toward others. Even after a divorce, parents should honor each other, visibly attaching high worth to even the offender by forgiving and releasing. Our children should see that *following Christ brings value* to everyone's life, including theirs, and that *they are protected* within the community of faith. And the world will take notice and be drawn to God through such love.

If there are issues that need to be resolved in your marriage, please talk to God about them right now. Ask Him for an opportunity to respectfully approach your spouse about them. Go with confidence and humility—confidence that God has a plan for correcting the situation, and humility that recognizes that some of the fault may be yours. It's like that *both* of you will need to change some attitude or behavior.

Whether married or single, if you are a follower of Jesus Christ, you are in a "family," the family of God. Will you pledge with me to begin to care more deeply for others in "the family" by preserving, cherishing, protecting, and honoring them—to the glory of God?

If so, answer "yes" below:

Chapter Six

The Defeat of Shame

Life has been hard for many of us. Now, even though we are followers of Jesus Christ, we may live with memories that are humiliating. What if our failures or sins haunt us even today? How do we get rid of these feelings of shame?

Jesus was born into a culture that attached shame to not only sin, but being poor, having physical deformities and disease, and merely being a Gentile or a woman. And there was shame for being haunted by demons that drove one mad.

I have learned a lot from the life of a special woman who was a contemporary of Jesus. Remember Mary Magdalene? In Luke 8:2, we find our one clue to Mary's past: Before Jesus set her free, she had been possessed by seven demons. If anyone had known shame, she had. We don't know how long the demons had tormented her, or whether they had caused physical deformity, mental insanity, or simply anguish of soul.

She may have lived in the tombs with other outcasts—begging for food, battered and broken. Or she may have been locked in a backroom of someone's home, in mental torment. Or she might have been wealthy, but trapped in a disease brought on by evil spirits.

Then Jesus came her way and he healed her! His love broke through her walls of shame. He didn't care what others thought of her or how far down she had sunk. Over and over, in order to reach men and women's hearts, Jesus disregarded all the rules that hold shame in place.

Set Free

Jesus set something new loose in the world—salvation that was inclusive, based on faith and grace! He didn't come to destroy the law, but to destroy its ability to exclude people from peace with God and drive them to despair. He proved that when God's love arrives, shame is defeated.

Jesus gave Mary Magdalene a new heart and a new life. Her mind was restored. Her spirit was made alive. She was washed clean and set free. From that day forward, she came out of hiding and followed him completely. She was like that other woman mentioned in Luke 7, who washed Jesus' feet with her tears and who loved much because she had been forgiven much. Both followed Jesus out of gratitude and love.

When Jesus was crucified, Mary's heart must have broken. The one who, above all others, knew her to be sane and whole was no more. The one who risked his own reputation to draw her out of hiding and include her with his closest followers was dead! I wonder if, in His absence, shame began its old attack. *Who am I without Jesus to follow? Will my madness return?* Satan loves to make us doubt our freedom.

Hope Restored

Mary must have been beside herself with joy when she saw that Jesus was alive again. When she saw Him free of her shame and standing gloriously before her, she knew that what He had accomplished in her heart was true and would last. He had taken her shame and buried it in hell where it belonged. She was free indeed!

Do you realize how amazing this is? Do you realize what it means to us today?

Jesus came to bring us *all* out of hiding. His love will destroy the pattern of shame that engulfs our lives. He calls everyone—outcasts included—to come to Him and be free. He will restore His glory to our lives.

Prophecy Fulfilled

Remember the time when Jesus went to the synagogue and declared His purpose in coming to earth by reading Isaiah's prophecy which they knew well? *The Spirit of the Lord is on me, because he has anointed me to preach good news to the poor. He has sent me to proclaim freedom for the prisoners and recover of sight for the* blind, *to release the oppressed, to proclaim the year of the Lord's favor.* (Luke 4:118-19)

Chills must have run up and down his hearers' spines. What would they do with a man who made such claims? While most were furious with him, maybe some of them sensed the nearness of the power and purpose of those scriptures for the very first time.

The promise and the challenge have not changed. He is here for us now saying, "You don't need to hide anymore! I will set you free."

Our Shame

We all bear shame—perhaps shame over sexual sin, a marriage that is falling apart, depression or fear, abortion or divorce, job losses, betrayal by a trusted friend or spouse, or failure as a parent.

But the shame and the lies we have believed about our worthlessness too often *stick* to us, becoming part of us. We know Jesus died for our sins and will forgive us, but we can't forgive ourselves, and we struggle to forgive others. We hide, or we exaggerate our goodness to make up for our shame. We judge in an attempt to spread the shame to others.

We need restoration. We need again the dignity of God that was on Adam and Eve in the beginning. And that's why Jesus came—to redeem us, to take upon Himself our sin and shame and give His life as a ransom for ours. He came to dispel the lie that we must be ashamed of ourselves forever. He came to forgive and heal us, to wash us clean and win our hearts.

No matter what we have experienced, those experiences don't have to define us anymore! When we see ourselves clean again this side of the resurrection, we will have the God-confidence to follow hard after Him!

Our Time for Restoration

We all try to look so perfect. But for many of us—maybe **all** of us—there is a tattered cloak of shame hidden under our nice clothes. Hanging onto our sorrows, failures, rebellion, stubbornness, control, withdrawal, or secrecy will not set us free nor restore His glory to our lives.

Right now, imagine taking off that decaying garment of shame. Give it to Jesus. *He will know what to do with it.* Give Him your regrets and disappointments, your failures and wounds—even your fatigue from caring for others. Listen to this encouragement from your heavenly Father:

If you think God has forgotten you, He answers in Isaiah 49:15: *"Can a mother forget the baby at her breast and have no compassion on the child she has borne? Though she may forget,* **I will not forget you!** *See, I have engraved you on the palms of my hands..."*

If you are a believer who has wandered far from Him, but you're asking His forgiveness right now, God says in Is. 44:21-22: *"I have swept away your offenses like a cloud, your sins like* the morning mist. Return to me, for I have redeemed you."

If you have been sexually abused, God says in Jeremiah 31:3-4: "I have loved you with an everlasting love; I have drawn you with lovingkindness. I will build you up again and you will be rebuilt, O Virgin Israel."

He also promises in Jeremiah 31:17: "I will restore you to health and heal your wounds," declares the Lord.

If you have been abandoned or betrayed by a spouse, God speaks through Isaiah 54:4-6 and says: "Do not be afraid; you will not suffer shame. Do not fear disgrace; you will not be humiliated. You will forget the shame of your youth and remember no more the reproach of your widowhood. For your Maker is your husband—the Lord Almighty is his name—the Holy One of Israel is your Redeemer; he is called the God of all the earth. The Lord will call you back as if you were a wife deserted and distressed in spirit—a wife who married young, only to be rejected," says your God.

The psalmist David assures us that The Lord is close to the brokenhearted and saves those who are crushed in spirit, Ps. 34:18. God Himself says: "I have called you by name; you are mine."

If you are weary in ministry and feel shame that your harvest seems very small right now, remember what Paul writes in Galatians 6:9: Let us not become weary in doing good, for at the proper time we will reap a harvest if we do not give up.

For all of us, it is written in Jeremiah 17:7-8: *Blessed is the man or woman who trusts in the Lord, whose confidence is in him. (S)he will be like a tree planted by the water that sends out its roots by the stream. It does not fear when heat comes; its leaves are always green. It has no worries in a year of drought and never fails to bear fruit.*

If you are a believer in Jesus Christ, but have been struggling with shame, pray right now:

"Dear Jesus, I confess I have hidden my shame deep inside. I have been angry at myself, those who have hurt me, and even You, Lord.

"I now receive your mercy and forgiveness for my sins, and I release mercy and forgiveness to those who have sinned against me, and bless them. Take my shame—my sins, wounds, weaknesses, sorrows, disappointments, and pride. I now fully embrace your love and acceptance that set me free at last. Wash me clean. Restore your glory to my life! Thank you, Jesus. Amen."

If you have not been a follower of Jesus Christ but want to turn your heart over to Him right now and begin experiencing His love and healing from shame, pray this prayer with me:

"Dear Jesus, I confess that my sins and shame have separated me from you. I want that separation to end! I now believe that you are the Son of God and that you love me. I accept your death as the payment for all my unbelief, hurt, and shame. Take my heart and make it new. From this day forward, I will trust in you.

"Thank you for your forgiveness and mercy. Help me to be merciful to others and forgive those who have sinned against me. Thank you, God, for loving me and making me your child. Amen!"

And now, Jesus is calling all of us to follow Him with abandonment and passion. Let's walk in faith with Him, as Mary did, and share with others that Jesus can restore His glory to their lives as well.

Will you say aloud with me these words of King David's? *I sought the Lord, and he answered me; he delivered me from all my fears. Those who look to him are radiant; their faces are never covered with shame.*

If you said those words aloud with me and sense that God has taken your shame and given you hope for the future, sign below:

_____(Your name)
_____(Today's date)

Praise God for this *Journey to Joy*!

Part 3

Living in Intimacy
with God

Chapter Seven

In His Presence

If there is one thing of which we can be sure, it is that we are loved by God. This is accepted at first by an act of faith, and then it is learned deeply by spending intentional time with Him. A story I heard several years ago about six-year-old Maria and her first daytrip to the woods with her dad reminds me of our own experiences of being with our *heavenly* Father.

It was a beautiful day, just right for exploring the wooded mountainside. The sun was shining down through the tree branches, and they were excited about what lay ahead.

The trail Maria's dad had chosen was both fascinating and difficult in places. Early in the day, Maria slipped on a tree root, twisting her ankle slightly, and had to be carried part of the way. But they pressed on. Since she was a very curious little girl, her papa had to warn her frequently about the dangers of the trail. "Don't touch that! It's poisonous!" or "Don't put your hand into that groundhog hole!" Twice he had to remove ticks from Maria's tender skin, which made the little girl cry. But most of the time, they laughed and told each other stories or simply soaked up the beautiful scenery in silence. They never tired of congratulating themselves on how far they had trekked.

At the end of the day, they both knew that it had been an adventure they'd never forget. As Papa drove home with his tired, but happy, daughter asleep beside him, peace flooded the vehicle. The trip has been a success for one simple reason—they had been together.

So it is with us and God. Our heavenly Father enjoys being with us, even if we have much to learn. *He loves us*, and His patience is limitless. Indeed, there's something about being in His company that gives us dignity, security, and a great sense of purpose. And we are no longer afraid to grow up.

A Common Roadblock

But what if we just can't seem to sense the presence of God even when we try to be close to Him? For any of us who have this problem, it may be hard to tell which comes first: Not believing that He loves us and, therefore, being unable to find intimacy with Him—or being unable to find intimacy with Him and, therefore, not believing that He loves us.

Could it be that no one has ever loved us unconditionally or expressed joy in simply spending time with us? That would certainly make it difficult to believe that *God* loves us and enjoys being with us. However, I have learned that great healing will come if we are willing to separate those who didn't know how to love us from our view of God—by forgiving them.

Through extending forgiveness, we will be released from our expectation that God will visit us with the same pain we have experienced at the hands of harsh human parents or other authority figures. God is like no one else! He will touch our hearts with His love when we forgive, and He will melt the stony barriers we erected when we were hurt before.

The Power of Forgiveness

One day a few years ago, I had lunch with a young woman who had just decided to follow Christ. While we were eating, Sarah told me that she was involved in a difficult lawsuit. She was suing her father for sexually abusing her as a child.

After hearing her story of suffering and anger, I asked her: "Do you believe that God loves you?" Tears began filling her eyes.

"I'm trying to believe that, but it's hard to imagine a heavenly Father being any different than my earthly father," Sarah admitted in dismay.

"God truly wants to heal your broken heart," I assured her. Then I asked her a simple question: "Is your revenge giving you freedom from what your father did to you?"

"No," she replied sadly, "I think about it all the time."

When I asked Sarah if she had ever thought of forgiving her father, she was visibly surprised.

"No one else has ever suggested that!" she exclaimed.

I then shared with her the power of forgiveness. Her heart was so ready to let go of the agony she had been carrying! She wept and asked God to take it all off her shoulders. She would give up the impossible task of making her father pay for his sins. As she forgave, God gave her peace. Best of all, she suddenly *knew* that God loved her perfectly, more perfectly than even the best of earthly fathers could.

The freedom and healing that forgiveness brought completely changed Sarah's view of her heavenly Father. She began to fall in love with Him.

More to the Story

After Sarah stopped the lawsuit, she began attending a Christ-centered church, and God continued setting her free from her past. After a few years, a miracle happened. God brought her father to that very church! After a lifetime of regret and misery, he had finally repented of his sins and surrendered his life to Christ, and now he was looking for a good place to worship. Sarah and her father had a somewhat awkward meeting in which he asked her to forgive him. She was able to tell him that she honestly had already forgiven him. God gave their relationship a new beginning, and their understanding of His love grew immensely.

Sarah's story is amazing! However, we must remember that not always will offenders repent when we forgive. But *even when they don't repent*, we can live free of bitterness and be at peace.

Getting to Know God

Jesus came to earth to show us what our heavenly Father is really like and to bring Him close (John 17:26). Jesus said that He did and said only what the Father told Him to, so we can study His behavior and teachings to understand the Father. The Holy Spirit, whom Jesus left with us when He returned to the Father, will reveal deep truths to us about the Father's loving and faithful intentions toward us.

The choice is ours. Yes, we can be His child and yet remain at a distance. But to do so will bring deep loneliness and confusion. To know Him from a distance is almost harder than if we had never met Him at all! We sense what we're missing, and if we stay away, the separation will eventually break both our hearts.

Even if we have been believers for many years, we may need to actively choose to trust Him today. If we have been living our lives at a distance from God, we must discover what we have let keep us away and resolve the problem.

For instance: Has someone offended us whom we have refused to forgive? An unwillingness to forgive will immediately erect a barrier between God and us. Or have we simply become too busy for God and left Him behind? We must go back to the place where we turned away from Him and humbly rejoin Him. On the other hand, have we been behaving in rebellious, selfish ways, caring nothing for those we hurt? Repentance is just a prayer and an apology away. As we set things right and return to His side, we will experience His love and peace once again.

Spending Time with Him

We must "practice His presence." This is indispensable. To "practice His presence" means that we are to live in the awareness that He is right there with us all the time and will guide us if we pay attention. It means inviting Him into every activity of our day and sharing it with Him whether we are at school, at home caring for our families, on a crowded bus, at the grocery store, at our jobs, at the dinner table, in our favorite quiet place where we read His Word, or in prayer and worship with other believers.

It's exciting to face life while fully engaged with Him. As we live life with Him, we begin to see events from His perspective. We are changed in the way we respond to the ups and downs that come our way. As we become "one" with Him, the needed transformation gains momentum.

Lifestyle of Intimacy

While it is crucial for us to practice His presence in each daily activity, it is vital to our spiritual, mental and emotional health to withdraw from busyness and the expectations of others to be alone with Him. It is when He has our undivided attention that our love for Him deepens and He straightens out the tangles of life.

In His presence, we grow in wisdom as His love finds our hearts; in His presence, we discover His strength in spite of our weakness; and in His presence, we find ourselves becoming more like His dear Son.

Let's pray together:

"Dear God, please help me more fully understand how much You love me. If there is something keeping me away from You, show me what it is. If I have believed that I am unworthy of love because of how someone else treated me in the past, help me forgive them (_____) just as You have forgiven me. You died on the cross for their sins too. And please separate my view of You from my view of them. I want a fresh start with You.

"I now invite You to be active in every area of my life. Go with me everywhere and impress Your thoughts upon my spirit. Teach me to face events with wisdom and grace.

"I also commit to spend exclusive time with You. Each day I will set aside a time and place to read about You in the Bible, talk to You, and invite You to speak to me. I want to know You more! In Jesus' name, amen."

Chapter Eight

The Art of Prayer

While prayer is quite simple, it is also amazing! Prayer is that two-way conversation with God that naturally happens as we practice His presence.

It's like breathing in and breathing out. We "breathe in" whatever He whispers to us through our experiences and His Word. In turn, we "breathe out" to Him our deepest thoughts and longings and ask for His wisdom for every aspect of our lives. Just as we cannot live without inhaling and exhaling air, we cannot sustain a healthy spiritual life without taking in His thoughts and giving Him ours.

An Analogy

Each of us desires a close relationship with God. But to illustrate how impossible it is to grow close to *anyone*—much less God—without this intimate exchange of heart, listen to the story a friend recently told me.

"When John and I first met, he sat and listened by the hour to my thoughts, hopes and dreams. He was so sensitive to me! As a result, I couldn't do enough for him.

"Then we got married. Suddenly, his interest in my life disappeared, and in the silence, I realized that we really barely knew each other. I felt as though I were living with a stranger.

"I tried to draw him out," she continued, "but that only irritated him. I remember shouting in frustration, 'You don't know me!'

"'Of course, I do!' he shouted back. 'I married you, didn't I?'"

My friend's husband just didn't get it. Consequently, each continued to feel alone, even while living in the same home. They had wedding rings on their fingers, but were essentially disconnected in spirit and soul.

Now, let's think about our relationship with God and the parallels to my friend's story. When we first met Jesus, remember how our hungry hearts devoured the Gospel and hung on His every word? And didn't we think about Him all the time? Remember how quickly we were convicted of sin, and how often our prayers were answered—sometimes even before we asked?

But now that we are "married" to Him and His ring is on our finger, do we sometimes lapse into expecting Him to be satisfied with a relationship in which we are distracted, distant, and self-absorbed? Have we stopped caring about what is important to Him? Have we taken intimacy with God for granted?

The truth is that God longs to speak *to* us and hear *from* us. Beth Moore, a well-known Bible teacher, said this once: "We must pray as though Jesus, in all His glory, were sitting across the table from us. We must pray knowing He hears." Knowing that He hears us grows out of practical, personal, daily fellowship with Him.

Powerful

If we will pursue Him honestly and tune our hearts to what matters to Him, the Holy Spirit will invade our prayers with His power. Soon our prayers will include not only our concerns for ourselves, but for others as well. Interceding—petitioning God on behalf of others—will invite God into the dire situations of their lives to move the mountains that stand in the way of their faith.

Prayer brings great change. Watchman Nee writes: *"Our prayers are the tracks on which the power of God travels."* The Bible tells us that this power is intensified when we join with one or more other persons. In Matt. 18:19-20, Jesus states: *"If two or more of you agree on earth concerning anything that they ask, it will be done for them by My Father in heaven."* He also says that *"...where two or three are gathered together in My name, I am there in the midst of them."*

Passion and Persistence

When I was a teacher at Teen Challenge, I asked the residents why they had given up drugs and alcohol and come to Christ.

Ninety percent said it was because of praying women in their families. Sisters, mothers and wives, your prayers are powerful! Fathers, join your wives in praying with passion and persistence for your children. Amazing things can happen!

But Satan wants to keep us unaware of our right to be personally involved with God. He also wants to prevent us from caring for one another in prayer. He knows that if we are fully surrendered to God and our prayers release the power of God, he, Satan, will be in deep trouble. When we resist the temptation to give up and, instead, persist in prayer, he has to flee.

Prepare for Battle

Following Christ has always been couched in struggle. It is an assault against the forces of evil. Jesus told His followers that taking the kingdom would be done by men and women who were willing to tear down Satan's strongholds. Their weapons and their protection would be the Word of Truth and the righteousness that comes from believing God. They would "turn the world upside down"—not the world of Caesar as was hoped for, but the world of Satan.

Satan was defeated at Calvary, even though he won't admit it. Be encouraged by that fact. He is no match for God! He is not the all-powerful, unstoppable force he wants us to believe he is. But because of his delusion of power, much struggle yet awaits the Church on its way to completely possessing the land.

What do I mean? Let's look at history for an illustration. Hitler's defeat in WW II gives us a good picture of Satan's true situation. In 1943, when Hitler's forces failed to take Stalingrad and Hitler was denied control of the Soviet Union, his defeat was basically settled. His power was broken and his forces demoralized.

But Hitler himself would not accept the defeat that the rest of the world knew to be sure—not until Berlin was taken in 1945. So for two long years after his defeat in Russia, the Allies still had to battle the remaining German soldiers and drive them out of each country, one by one, because Hitler simply wouldn't admit defeat. His delusion of power was so great that he kept sending boys into battle even though everyone knew there was no chance of victory. Hitler was determined to wound and maim men and women on both sides of the conflict as long as he had breath.

Likewise, today, we must drive the forces of our spiritual enemy out of our lives, homes and communities, taking back the ground that was given him through unbelief. Even though we know his doom was sealed when Jesus died and rose again, he will keep fighting us rather than face the truth.

And how will we know how to wage this war? By praying. Spirit-led prayer is the deciding factor in spiritual conflict. It exposes deception and moves the hand of God. It is the power source to win back the hearts of our family members and bring victory in the deepest areas of our lives.

When we know His will, we will go before Him with great boldness. What He wants, we then want! When we know His Word, we can speak it with authority to resist Satan and his lies. Prayer makes us partners with God and releases His power into the circumstance to accomplish His will.

The Holy Spirit who dwells within every believer knows God's perfect will (Romans 8:26-27). And when we are not sure how to pray, or are at our weakest in the battle, we can invite the Holy Spirit to pray through us. We can say this: "Holy Spirit, pray through me the things the Father wants done. Father, I agree with whatever the Spirit within me is praying. In Jesus' name, I offer this prayer. May what you desire be fully done in this situation." Best of all, Jesus Himself is in heaven interceding for us (Romans 8:34)!

A Personal Example

Two nights before teaching on this subject for the first time, I had a terrible experience. I felt utterly abandoned by God. It was the worst and most desolate feeling in the world. I felt disconnected from my very life and everything around me. There suddenly seemed to be no purpose to anything.

I began to search my heart for the source of this strange thinking. Was there unforgiveness or bitterness in my heart that could be blocking God's presence and giving Satan permission to torture me? No, there wasn't. Was I being disobedient to God in some way? No again. I then realized that it was a frontal attack by Satan.

So, I proceeded to pray in the Spirit. Before long, the Holy Spirit gave me a plan. He prompted me to begin thanking God for every time I had ever felt His presence in the past, every time I had seen Him act in my life. Before I could finish describing all those times and thanking Him for them, I was sleeping peacefully. In the morning, the feeling of desolation was gone and the presence of God was all around me. Praying in the Spirit had been the key to finding the way to defeat Satan and drive away the sense of desolation and abandonment.

Remain Confident

Let me warn you, however: Don't be surprised when the enemy whispers into your ear, "Who do you think you are that God would hear and answer your prayers? You don't deserve anything from God!"

Satan will haunt us with the evidence of our unworthiness and, therefore, the uselessness of our praying. As a result, instead of speaking boldly in simple trust to the living God, we may draw back, feeling as though we are trying to get a favor from someone we've just insulted! Satan hopes that we will forget that we can come boldly through *Christ's* righteousness. Christ's death and resurrection broke down every wall that could separate us from God. We can come into His presence with confidence and speak freely whatever is on our hearts.

And when times look the darkest, remember that nothing happens for the blessing of mankind without a struggle. Jesus struggled gravely in Gethsemane. Luke 22:41-44 says: *He pulled away from them about a stone's throw, knelt down, and prayed, "Father, remove this cup from me. But please, not what I want. What do **you** want?"* *He prayed on all the harder. Sweat, wrung from him like drops of blood, poured off his face.* (The Message) In the power of prayer, He prevailed, and so will we. We are authorized by God Himself to transact business against the enemy through prayer.

Taking Our Stand

Lynn Sparks, a discerning intercessor and friend of mine, likes to say: "Spiritual warfare is like drawing a line in the sand and telling Satan he has gone too far and can advance no further. It's telling him we are prepared to fight over this specific territory and take back what he has stolen. In Ephesians 6, we are called to 'stand'. It's announcing to Satan that we will stand in faith against him and his schemes.

"The only offensive weapon we are given to do this is the sword of the Spirit, which is the Word of God. Scripture acts like a two-edged sword that can reveal the truth which then can be used to overcome the lies of the enemy. Satan typically attacks God's character and our value. When the attacks come, we can set the enemy to flight by quoting scripture that asserts God's love and faithfulness and our position as His children."

All the rest of the equipment cited in Ephesians 6:10-18 is defensive protection. The belt of truth protects the depths of our lives, our very souls. The breastplate of righteousness (believing God) protects our hearts. Feet prepared and unafraid to hold their ground cause the gospel of peace to advance. The helmet of salvation protects our minds from being penetrated by Satan's lies. Finally, the shield of our faith repels Satan's accusing words, rendering them harmless.

As Paul concludes this passage in Ephesians, he urges us to pray in the Spirit on all occasions, with all kinds of prayers and requests, and to remember to pray for other believers. We are in this battle together and need to cover each other's back.

The Promise

All of us can communicate freely with the living God. This privilege is not limited to a special few. God doesn't have favorites. As we surrender every area of our lives to Jesus Christ and invite the Holy Spirit to fill us and to speak to us through the Word, we will receive the discernment for intercession and the power we live in victory.

I love Jeremiah 29:11 where He says to His people, *"For I know the plans I have for you, plans to prosper you and not to harm you, plans to give you hope and a future."* King James Version says, *"...to give you an expected end"* which quite literally means "to give you what you long for." This is a promise from God. He goes on to say that when we call on Him and pray unto Him, he will listen to us. He asks us to trust Him to execute that plan and bring it to pass.

The key is to long for what *He* longs for. This only comes from intimate fellowship with Him in prayer and in the Word every day.

I want to close with the words of David in Psalm 20:4-5 as a blessing for you as you learn to desire what He desires and center your life in Him.

May He give you the desire of your heart and make all your plans succeed. We will shout for joy when you are victorious and will lift up our banners in the name of our God. Amen!

What are your spiritual desires? What do you believe God wants to do in your life? What battles must be won? Record those desires and beliefs here and then pray with confidence:

_____

_____

_____

_____

_____

_____

_____

_____

_____

_____

May God's Kingdom come and His will be done in your life!

Chapter Nine

Unspeakable Joy

Jesus wants our love and devotion, but He will not demand them. They can only be given as a gift. Mary, who lived with her sister Martha and her brother Lazarus in Bethany (Luke 10), gave Him this gift long ago. It happened when Jesus and His disciples stopped at her home for a surprise visit. Here's how I think she would have told us her story:

"It seemed an odd time to do nothing. Jesus and all twelve of His disciples dropped in on us unexpectedly, and just at mealtime! Martha sprang into action to fix dinner and serve the men, and normally, I would have done the same.

"But something unexplainable gripped my heart and made me unable to leave Jesus' side. I didn't want to miss a moment with Him.

"Martha was, of course, furious that I wasn't helping her, and perhaps the disciples were annoyed too, although they didn't express it. After all, women were supposed to serve the men and then stay out of sight—not be part of serious discussions in the living room! But right then, I didn't care what they thought. To be with Jesus meant more to me

than the dictates of custom or the demands of the moment.

"As I sank to the floor at His feet, He shifted slightly on His mat to give me more room, His face breaking into a smile. The disciples—forever trying to adjust to Jesus' unpredictable behavior—felt awkward but said nothing. I kept my eyes fixed on Him. He alone could send me away...and He didn't!

"As He talked of Kingdom matters—of life and death and the heart of His Father—I listened, taking in every word and weighing its meaning. It seemed important that I, just as much as the disciples, grasp His mission and how it would affect our lives. There was a long journey ahead for all who followed Him, and we all needed to know that He would give us direction and strength.

"There in His presence, no matter what lay ahead, I was at peace. As I gave Him the gift of my love and devotion, He in return filled every empty space in my life with His love and drew me into His world. Soldiers could have broken down the door and put us in chains and I wouldn't have been afraid!

"Best of all, He was very pleased that I had spent that time with Him. He even told Martha that He wished she had left the work behind and done the same. I feel sorry for her that she missed all that I enjoyed.

"That day, food wasn't on His mind; that day only our relationship was worth spending time on. That I chose Him over labor blessed us both so much!"

Today

And so it is with us today. In His presence, we remember our reason for living and the worth of it all. In His presence, we are healed in mind, will and emotions time and time again. As we worship Him deeply, He ministers to us, clearing our vision so that we can see the victory close at hand even when we've nearly lost hope. As we listen closely to what He whispers into our spirits, His purposes are revealed. In His presence, we fall in love with Him all over again! Service follows when the time is right, but sensitivity to what comes first is an important lesson to learn.

God Speaks

There are, unfortunately, many people who don't believe that God communicates with people today. But let me assure you, *God does speak.* Every spiritual mile in my life has been marked by His voice. I would like to share some of them with you to encourage you to listen for yourself.

Through Words: The first time I clearly heard his voice was one special night at a Christian summer camp when I was 14 years old. My heart was pounding as I sensed God telling me that I would someday go to foreign lands to teach and encourage believers. At the time, I wondered how it could ever come to be.

As the years passed and I grew into an adult, the memory of that episode grew dim. I nearly forgot about it, but He didn't. In 1996, the first invitation came from Russia, and I have been back nearly every year for the past twelve years. In 2002 and 2003, invitations came from India; in 2008, from Bermuda and England as well. As long as doors are open and invitations come, I will go wherever God leads.

Before the very first trip to Russia, I cried out to God, "What will I say to them?" He spoke again, this time through Ps. 32:8—*I will instruct you and teach you in the way you should go; I will counsel you and watch over you.* I go each time totally aware of what He wants me to teach and at peace in His presence. I trust Him because He has kept His promise all these years. I assure you that when God speaks, He means what He says.

Through Impressions: The next time He spoke to me, He didn't use words. I was in my senior year of college, and I was begging God to show me that He was real and could do supernatural things. One night, I just happened to look in on a gathering of students where David Wilkerson, founder of Teen Challenge, was excitedly telling incredible stories of how he had seen the Spirit of God supernaturally deliver young men from drug and alcohol addiction. At that very moment, as I sat in the shadows at the back of the auditorium, I begged God to verify that what I was hearing was true. Immediately, the Holy Spirit wrapped me in what felt like a warm blanket and assured me that He truly was a miracle-working God! I left the building and walked rapidly out into the clear, cold night, shouting to the star-filled sky, "He's real! He's real!"

Several years later, I found myself teaching at the very rehabilitation center in the hills of Pennsylvania that David Wilkerson had founded. How amazing is that?

Through His Powerful Presence: As a young mom, I remember hungering to be filled with the power of the Holy Spirit in a deeper way than ever before. He answered my cry this time by invading my life with such power that I could not stand up for nearly half an hour. It was as though He had walked in the front door and filled me with His presence. I had been taught little about the Holy Spirit while I was growing up, but I learned that night that He is a very real person who wants to fill each of us with His power so that our lives can be used to make a wonderful difference in the world.

Through Visions: Several years after that experience, the Holy Spirit spoke to me through visions in the middle of the night, warning me that I was on dangerous ground in a certain relationship. I had needed something graphic to get my attention. Nine months later, He showed me all the arrogance and ungratefulness that had been collecting in my heart because I had not let His love satisfy me completely. This led to a level of repentance that radically changed my life.

Through Others: Another time He spoke to me through my husband. He told Jim that I must turn down a lucrative job offer and, instead, ask God what *He* wanted me to do, whether it paid any money or not. This was extremely hard to understand because Jim was out of work at the time, and we were in desperate need financially. But God wanted to teach us both something new about trusting

Him. So with some trepidation, I agreed to refuse the job and began to seek *God's* purpose.

How did God reward us for our obedience? By the end of the day, God had clearly impressed me to begin writing my first book, with many more to follow. Then two days later, right after I rejected the teaching job, Jim was offered his first church administration position, in Sarasota, Florida. With no previous church administration experience, he was chosen over 200 qualified applicants. God changed the direction of both our lives through that one act of obedience.

Through the Bible: After two years of writing and trying to find a publisher for that first book, I desperately needed to hear from Him again. With tears of frustration, I cried out to God, "When will all my labor pay off?" He responded with Jeremiah 31:16—*This is what the Lord says: "Restrain your voice from weeping and your eyes from tears, for your work will be rewarded," declares the Lord.*

Lambs on the Ledge is now published not only in English, but in Portuguese, Chinese, and Russian. What a wonderful reward! Furthermore, my original publisher told me that it would be a classic—a book that would be read for generations to come.

Always There

God is in the midst of every part of your life and mine. He is in the midst of every exciting and fruitful season—but also of the winters when all seems dead and still. During those dark seasons, He sits with us, grieves with us, and comforts us—sometimes soundlessly. But He's there as only a best friend can be.

God *will* speak to us. He will speak through a million images and events around us and through His Word, even when His voice seems silent. He will speak before we are willing to obey, but we would be foolish *not* to obey!

Stay Close

Remember, we don't have to earn the right to hear His voice. This loving relationship is freely given. But when our hearts are far from Him, we may walk right past Him, hear nothing, and even wonder where He's gone!

And when we come stumbling back to Him, He doesn't punish us. He simply asks, "Where have you **been**?" Not because He doesn't know, but because we need to confront and abandon what had drawn us away.

The Truth

Let's invite Him into every area of our lives. Let's also wisely set aside life's demands and others' expectations to spend specific time with Him. This is critical, not optional. If we neglect being with Him in personal worship and devotion—if we are instead too busy performing—we will soon run out of spiritual insight and energy.

If we do not spend time meditating on what He says in the Bible, we will eventually lose our way. As Psalm 119:33-35 and 103-105 says: *Teach me, O Lord, to follow your decrees; then*

I will keep them to the end. Give me understanding, and I will keep your law and obey it with all my heart. Direct me in the path of your commands, for there I find delight. How sweet are your words to my taste, sweeter than honey to my mouth! I gain understanding from your precepts; therefore I hate every wrong path. Your word is a lamp to my feet and a light for my path.

Wisdom for the journey is found in His Word. No matter how many times we read even the same passage, the Holy Spirit will bring it to life for us in new ways. It becomes the "food" that feeds our spirits and keeps us from sin. In His Word we are reminded of the mighty acts God has performed for those who loved Him down through history. We also find practical instruction for how to live each day. We discover the truth that dispels the lies of Satan. We learn how to forgive and how to go to others for forgiveness so that our relationships can be healed. We receive warning about the dangers of compromise. In God's Word, we find encouragement when we are treated unjustly; we find that Jesus experienced such treatment too and forgave. Best of all, we encounter Him.

You see, we cannot live sanely without Him, and we cannot endure to the end without hearing from Him.

Without His life within us by faith, we are of little consequence. Simply as human beings, our lives are fragile and short—like grass that withers and the flower that fades. However, when we become His children by inviting Him to be our Father, we are given eternal life through His Son—life that changes us now and forever. This relationship becomes an amazing adventure which doesn't end at physical death! After we leave this earth, we will be with Him forever, because our souls will never die. He has promised that where He is, there we will be, whether here by His Spirit who lives within us or face to face in heaven someday.

As we determine to walk with Him here on this earth, worship will refresh us, and reading the Bible will feed our souls. Prayer will become a natural two-way conversation that gives deep direction to our lives, and we will feel as though we are sitting at His feet just as Mary was.

Best of all, this journey will take us "home"—home to the God who loves us and is waiting to establish our identity as His beloved child, unite us in love with one another, and reveal the spiritual purposes for our lives. As we are changed in God's presence, others will be inspired to invite Him to change them as well. And they will join us on this amazing *Journey to Joy*.

As we come to the end of this journey together, will you accept God's invitation to know Him and spend time with Him on a highly personal level? If your answer is "yes," please sign your name below and record the date.

_____(Your name)
_____ (Today's date)

How will you rearrange your priorities tomorrow to spend time with God in prayer, meditation on the Scriptures, and listening for what He might be saying to you?

_____

_____

_____

_____

_____

And, the final question: Are you willing to pay the cost of obedience? _____

Let's pray together:

"Dear Lord, as I spend time with you each day, please give me a sense of your presence and how much you love me. Give me direction for my life and teach me how to pray effectively. Help me persist in prayer so that others will come to know you too.

"I love you, Lord, and I love the wonderful changes you are making in my life. Thank you for taking me on this profound *Journey to Joy!*"

Other Books by Joyce Strong

Lambs on the Ledge: Seeing and Avoiding Danger in Spiritual Leadership

Caught in the Crossfire: Confronted by the Uncompromising, Compassionate Love of God

Instruments for His Glory: Women Ministering in Harmony with God and Man

Leading with Passion and Grace: Encouraging and Mentoring Women Leaders in the Body of Christ

Of Dreams and Kings and Mystical Things:
A Biblical Novel on the Life of King David

A Dragon, A Dreamer, and the Promise Giver:
A Biblical Novel on the Life of King Solomon

To learn more about the author, comment on this book, or invite Joyce to speak, visit her website: www. joycestrongministries.org